Franky, the Cranky Crab

Written and Illustrated
by
Mary Sayers

Matchstick Literary
1-888-306-8885
orders@matchliterary.com

This book is dedicated to my parents,
Frank and Clarice, who discovered they were
a perfect match many years ago.

It was a blistering day at the beach when Franky, a little **RED** crab first crawled out of a dark hole near the water,

"I can't see! I can't see!" cried the cranky little crab as he scurried back to the coolness of his damp home in the sand. "The sun is too bright, and the sand is so hot. It is cooking my claws like stew in a pot" he whined.

"Oh, no you don't," scolded Mama with a snap of her claw. "Out you go for a run in the warm summer sun. Find a friend, build a castle; try to have fun!" she said scooting him back outside.

As soon as Franky the cranky crab stepped outside again, his shell turned bright yellow just like the sun. The hot YELLOW crab covered his eyes and scampered down the beach.

Soon, Franky the hot yellow crab spotted some sandpipers playing along the shore. "What are you doing?" he asked the small birds. "Racing," yelled the first bird. "We're trying to beat the waves back to the beach," called his friend.

"Let's run and have some fun!" chirped the birds chasing him into the very cold water. "It's freezing!" Franky screamed as he shivered, and his shell turned white like the wave caps rolling in from the sea. The sandpipers laughed. "Run! Run!" they shouted, so the cold WHITE crab beat the waves back to the shore and quickly scampered down the beach.

Before long, Franky the cold white crab saw a huge brown rock sitting in the sand. He hooked his large front claw to the rock, and pulled himself up to bask in the warm sunlight. As soon as he sat down, the rock stood up,

"Yyyou are nnnot a rock at all" Franky stuttered. "No, I am not" snapped the angry lobster with a flip of his tail. "Up, up you go as high as the sun, and when you land you'd better run!" he warned.

Franky went flying through the air and landed with a thud. As the scared little crab brushed sand off his shell, he saw that it was the same color as the lobster. "I'm sore and I don't feel very well" he moaned. Without looking back, the scared **BROWN** crab quickly scampered down the beach.

After a while, Franky the scared brown crab saw a large lump of grape jelly stuck in the sand. He squatted on his empty belly and scooted slowly to the jelly.

By this time the little crab felt very hungry. He thought he must be starving, so he poked his claw into the shiny purple blob. "Ouch! That hurt," Franky shouted quickly pulling back his stinging purple claw. "All I wanted was something to eat," cried the hurt little crab.

"Sure you did," blurted the bubble. "How would you like to be a helpless jellyfish stuck in the sand waiting for any little crab that comes along to eat you?" he yelled. "Leave me be or you will see, it won't be fun if twice you're stung," So, the pouty **PURPLE** crab dried his eyes and carefully scampered down the beach.

By midday, Franky the pouty purple crab was very, very hungry. Feeling faint, the dizzy crab drifted down the beach and got tangled in some seaweed.

I'm as hungry as a whale he thought, and dropped down in the pile of seaweed to chew on the salty green leaves. The more he chewed the greener he grew. By the time he finished, Franky was as green as the seaweed and feeling rather ill. So, the sick GREEN crab wiped off his shell and slowly scampered down the beach.

By now, Franky the sick green crab had walked far from home and was lost. Eating so much made him tired; it was time to find someplace safe to sleep. While looking for a quiet place to spend the night, he spotted the crown of a conch shell half-covered with sand.

At first, Franky was afraid to get too close, but he quietly tiptoed to the front of the shell and peeked inside.

"Is anyone home?" called the lost little crab. He listened for an answer, but hearing only the sound of the ocean, Franky slowly turned around and scooted backwards into the cozy orange shell.

Lost, tired and all alone, he tucked in his claws and never even noticed that his color had changed again. As day turned to dusk, the tired **ORANGE** crab snuggled tightly and fell fast asleep on the beach.

Later that night a storm blew in. ZAP! A lightning bolt struck the shell making Franky jump with a jolt. A loud crack of thunder rumbled. Cold rain dropped down drenching the shocked little crab. He was soaked to the shell.

As Franky sat sobbing on the beach, he watched his body turn as blue as the raindrops. Wet and weary, the lonely little crab drifted in and out of sleep. Franky dreamed about returning to his damp sandy home by the ocean where he had many friends, so the sad **BLUE** crab closed his eyes once more and slept for hours on the beach.

When morning came, the rain stopped. "Wake up!" Franky the sad, blue crab heard a soft, gentle voice say. "I'm Clarice. Who are you?" she asked. Sleepily, the little blue crab opened his eyes and saw a cute red crab smiling down at him. She was so kind and friendly that he forgot all about feeling sad and blue.

"I'm Franky," he said. He told her all about being lost and not feeling like himself lately. "I walked down the beach all day changing colors along the way," he explained. Franky stood up and scurried closer to Clarice. "So you see I may be blue, but once upon a time I was red like you."

Clarice smiled and replied, "I know! I've watched your colors come and go. I think you have turned every color in a rainbow." At last, Franky found a new friend who admired all of his bold colors. Clarice loved his color blue, and how it matched the ocean's hue.

She also loved him wearing orange because it made her heart feel warm.

Clarice was amazed when Franky soared high, and turned chocolate brown against the pink sky.

"Running white along the shore made you sparkle even more...

...but, back when you first changed to yellow, that's when I knew you were my fellow," she whispered.

Clarice gently wrapped her arms around her charming new friend and gave him a great big hug. "Without some rain, there can be no rainbow," she said "and I like all the colors of the rainbow."

"Me, too!" agreed Franky, and instantly the little **RED** crab was back!

"You color my world," Franky shouted with delight! Together, the happy little crabs clutched their claws and off they scampered down the beach.

Mary Sayers was born in Youngstown, Ohio and as a young girl moved to Florida with her family. She is now a mother and grandmother who keeps busy as an elementary school librarian, and believes a love for the **ABC**s: **A**rt, **B**ooks, and **C**hildren inspire her to write.

CPSIA information can be obtained
at www.ICGtesting.com
Printed in the USA
LVHW071414220520
656301LV00012B/1090